jewels of summer

clare ferguson

recipes for the best of british summer fruits

First published in Great Britain 2002

Published and produced for National Summer Fruits Ltd
By Grub Street Publishing
The Basement
10 Chivalry Road
London
SW11 1HT
post@grubstreet.co.uk
www.grubstreet.co.uk

Text and photographs © National Summer Fruits Ltd, 2002
Recipes created by Clare Ferguson
Food Styling for photography by Clare Ferguson
Assistant Pippa Cuthbert
Photographs by Michelle Garrett
Fruit Map © Dylan Woolf Photography
Design by ENVY
Introduction by Joan Cremer
Edited by Anne Dolamore
Colour origination by Saturn Graphics
Printed and bound in Spain by Bookprint, S.L.

ISBN 1904010229

contents

foreword

Everyone adores the taste of fresh fruit, and fragrant sun-ripened soft fruits are particularly gorgeous. These fruits astonish you with their utter perfection. These are the original, absolute fast foods. They existed long before labels and logos. Long before the dawn of manufacturing and vitamin pills.

British strawberries and raspberries; red, black and white currants; gooseberries, blackberries, plums and cherries are no exception: they have been famous for centuries.

The chance to create some new, deliciously easy recipes using British soft and stone fruits was a challenge too enjoyable to resist when I was offered it last year.

We should prize these lovely foods, particularly fresh, eaten in our fingers. We should have fun with them and never forget how to use them at home. Eat them raw, fresh and straight from the source if possible but, now that they can be found for many months on supermarket shelves in peak condition it is good to make the most of their countless charms, their easy versatility, every day, in lively, easy dishes, cooked as well as raw.

Think of soft fruits as nature's little bonus. These foods not only delight all our senses but are of immense benefit to our short-term and long-term wellbeing. They keep us active and fit and help protect us from illness as well as being a beauty plus. Not only do fruits contain the best kind of natural sweetness but they contain vitamins, minerals, useful anti-oxidants, bio-flavenoids, fruit acids and pectins as well as many other micro-nutrients, some of which are believed to delay ageing.

First of all, eyes wide: revel in their colour and beauty before all else. Savour any scents they may have. Touch their surfaces, explore their textures, enjoy their size. Now open your mouth. Nibble, bite, savour and swallow. Smile: a complex adventure in flavour has once again come your way.

Ready-made food products have used fruit flavours for appeal for centuries but we have become so used to buying industrially produced soft drinks, ice creams and syrups; cakes, pastries, preserves and pickles; jams, jellies and desserts, as well as main course dishes that we sometimes forget how good they are freshly prepared and how easy it is to make them at home. When did you last make a fruit cordial? Concoct a cocktail? Freeze your own berry ice? Create a soft fruit salsa? Bake a berry muffin? Cook up a pork, chicken or fish dish fragrant with the freshness of fruit for a quick weekday dinner?

This book may help encourage you to try some fruit-based dishes, easily created at home. You have nothing to lose but your inhibitions and everything to gain from the delicious goodness of these superb fruits and the pleasure they bring.

Cheers and bon appétit.

introduction

Britain has the perfect climate to grow and produce the best-flavoured soft and stone fruit in the world.

The title of this exciting new recipe book, *Jewels of Summer* sums up the very essence of the unique quality and superior flavour of Britain's seasonal soft and stone fruits. Its freshness and succulence is always eagerly awaited by consumers as a signal to the beginning of summer.

This book tells the story of a modern and vibrant industry producing the most delicious British fruits that are as versatile to cook but taste just as good eaten raw. They are truly the ultimate in healthy fast food.

British glasshouse strawberries get the season underway in mid-April and with the virtue of their distinct colour and texture remind consumers that summer is fast approaching. There has been a considerable increase in recent years of outdoor tunnel protection that ensures whatever the weather, British fruit is always available from early spring right through until late autumn.

Whilst the Wimbledon Tennis Championships, eternally linked with the famous British strawberry, are one reminder of a special treat, we are lucky in having many more fruits that can just as easily provide a tasty snack, a feast or a luscious pudding in next to no time.

British raspberries are the second most popular summer fruit and with such a wide range of varieties there is a wonderful array of aromatic flavours to choose from. They are a favourite for making memorable desserts and sauces and are excellent for freezing.

These two fruits are the very heart of the soft fruit industry but there are also plentiful supplies of British plums, cherries, gooseberries, blackberries and red and black currants that can be used for entertaining, easy family meals or just plain self indulgence. Whatever the choice, all these fruits are a symbol of freshness, health and a feeling of summer goodness that is hard to beat.

Superior produce quality is paramount and so growers pick the fruit in the field, quickly cool it before it is packed into punnets and distributed to supermarkets within hours. As well as offering British summer fruit for almost nine months of the year growers use their wealth of knowledge and expertise to keep up with consumer buying trends and also contribute to research into new British varieties. Both growers and supermarkets acknowledge consumers are keen to know where the produce comes from and so another innovation is to label the soft fruit punnet with its specific producer.

Supporting growers both in financial and practical terms are the individual marketing groups that are responsible for selling the fruit to supermarkets and other outlets. They provide a central organisation and perform the vital role of linking the distribution network with the challenges of having a cohesive voice for the industry. The largest soft fruit-marketing group in the Britain is KG Fruits based in Kent. KG represents soft and stone fruit growers from all over the United Kingdom and markets in excess of thirteen thousand tons of British fruit. Supermarkets, caterers and independent greengrocers are all supplied with daily deliveries of fresh fruit throughout the British season.

Sustaining all this hard work is the final and most important link in the production line, the supermarket. Their support and promotion means consumers are offered an array of quality British fruit that is well presented with eye-catching displays often connected to special tasting sessions.

Through the generosity of Marks & Spencer's part sponsorship of this book, the soft fruit industry has been enabled to get closer to consumers and to show the high standard of growing skills required to produce safe quality fruit. Marks & Spencer puts a great deal of time and effort into working closely with growers to maintain these carefully thought out working practices to ensure superb British fruit is always available to their customers.

This unique British cookbook combines all the elements of fruit growing with an insight into the individual fruit's distinct flavour, colour, shape and texture. The stunning recipes are a testament to their undoubted quality and versatility and will certainly bring delight, pleasure and some surprises proving British soft and stone fruits to be the real Jewels of Summer.

a passion for fruit

Soft and stone fruits are some of life's great treats. They give us gorgeous frothy blossoms in spring, luminous leaves then fragrant ripe, juicy fruits in summer and even autumn. Strawberries, raspberries, blackberries, currants, gooseberries, cherries and plums: these are sensational foods. They are delicious, beautiful and versatile – a huge success story. That these lovely fruits can today be raised, ripened, picked and packed into convenient containers and arrive at your local Marks & Spencer stores in a perfect, ripe-to-eat state seems like an everyday miracle. That they grow in ecologically responsible systems is satisfying, following an age old tradition.

But such things don't happen without centuries of agricultural expertise; decades of research and development and the intelligent use of friendly technology, along with amazingly efficient storage, distribution and transport systems.

National Summer Fruits is passionately keen to bring us the best there is. This book celebrates this achievement. The recipes which follow are alive with flavour, colour, vitality and goodness.

Grower-producers, the marketing co-operatives and Marks & Spencer are working closely in this exciting British enterprise. The wish is to produce and promote the most perfect, succulent, flavourful, beautiful and nutrient-packed soft fruits possible, and have these available on the produce shelves in a fraction of the time they took to produce. It's now possible to enjoy British soft fruits within hours of them leaving their fields, farms and orchards, their tunnels and glasshouses.

Amazingly, many of these fruits will never have been handled by any human fingers other than your own. Stem-picking and the newest technology ensure that you have the pleasure of the very first touch. What an achievement. Fruit cooling technology, heat-sealed punnet methods, which prevent accidental or tamper, damage help produce strawberries and raspberries in peak condition all season long. This brings the delights of the country to village, town and city dwellers from John O' Groats to Land's End. The country's own produce cherished and consumed in the land of its origin; a worthwhile aim.

Top fruit, soft fruit, stone fruit; plants, bushes, canes or trees: the wonderful world of British soft fruit may sound complex, but in reality, the moment you put a velvety-soft, crimson

raspberry between your lips or nibble a sensational scarlet strawberry or pull jewel-like currants from their fragile stems or have cherry or plum juice trickle down your chin or let blackberries stain your lips, you are entering one of the culinary world's greatest pleasure zones.

'That takes the cherry!' Here is a fond reference to the excellence of one of the world's best-known fruits: shiny red cherries. These look like perfect tree decorations hanging on their long stems between the serrated leaves. Though Sweetheart is a late-season variety there are also early-season Hertford, Van and Stella, main-season Sunburst, Summit, Lapins and Colney to revel in. Fresh or cooked, in cocktails, drinks, sauces or with main-dish meats cherries are nothing short of wonderful, and their nutrient line-up is impressive. Just as well that grower's nets ensure that the birds don't get them first.

'To be the gooseberry' is probably a fond dig at the sour-sweet appeal of a ripe gooseberry: these ancient fruits have always been cherished for their complexity. Pricking your fingers and scratching your arms as you skirmish for berries among the prickles of a thriving gooseberry bush is probably, too, part of the love-hate equation. How convenient that lovely translucent, green or rosy-veined, gooseberries can now be collected in neat little packs at your neighbourhood store. Gooseberries, known in Britain since Henry VIII's time, were once called fayberries. Fairies were believed to take shelter in these bushes and the juice was a popular medicine. The season from June through to August provides these versatile fruits, long useful in pastries and pudding, as the basis of jams, jellies and fools. They make superb, sharp sauces to match oily fish and roast pork and can be terrific in freshly made salsas and salads.

Plums, long the stuff of legend, ditties, fairy tales, poetry and songs are as much part of our everyday food world as are potatoes, even if we are unaware of their useful charms. Nearly every savoury brown sauce in your local chip shop or the chutney added to your 'ploughman's' sandwich at the local pub or the jam on many a hotel breakfast tray will contain plums, and at country fairs and farmers' markets throughout Britain we pounce upon plum preserves and pickles whenever we see them. Sugar plum fairies, plum cake, plum pudding, plum duff: it comes as no surprise that plum stones are regularly excavated from ancient archaeological sites, here and world wide. British plums were brought here from Syria and Persia by a member of the Gage family. Victoria and Damson are favourites but did you realise that Opal, Reeves, Avalon, Jubileum, Marjorie's Seeding along with Sanctus Hubertus are also available dessert plum varieties? So-called culinary varieties with a sharper taste are often utilised in the traditional cooked dishes, but dessert plums cook well even so.

Blackberries, wild in the hedgerows, or those grown on elegant canes, can be of two types. There's the North

American type such as the Silvan and Helen varieties fruiting early (July into late August) along with Kotata, which continues well into September, and the European type such as Loch Ness which come in from early August to late October. So from July to November we can have blackberries and cream, smoothies galore, blackberry and apple tarts, jams, jellies, crimson coulis and blackberry pavlovas whenever we choose. Bliss.

Once upon a time it was September only when we raided the roadside hedges and wild hillsides for brambles and, unless you had Wellington boots, gloves and long arms, you'd not always succeed. Helen and Adrienne, two exciting new varieties of North American lineage, were specifically developed into hugely successful British cultivars. The taste of a good blackberry, mashed between tongue, teeth and lips has an intense lush sweetness but with nice acidity and a lasting effect on the palate.

Fresh blackberries, in my view, are overdue for a revival. Their fascinating colour, taste and effect in all sorts of dishes from savoury to sweet, in drinks and in salads, as cooked glazes, sauces and garnishes, especially for game, makes them really valuable. Their nutrient profile is a bonus so blackberries mashed, with or without icing sugar, into live yogurt must be one of the best breakfasts possible and the easiest.

Gem-like red, white and black currants, though sharp and refreshing when eaten fresh and glorious when used as a garnish, are mainly used in Britain for juice production since they sing with vitamin C and they have strong medicinal benefits. Currants were used in cooking as far back as 1576 and probably came from Holland, Denmark and around the Baltic. Selective breeding has extended the season of these glamorous little fruits so you can revel in adding them to fresh fruit salads, long drinks, cooked and chilled desserts, jams, jellies and as salad garnishes.

What would summer be without strawberries and raspberries? These, the biggest sellers, are also the best-loved. Eaten in the fingers they cannot be beaten. They have unique versatility in all sorts of desserts, drinks, preserves, sauces, baking or with meat, poultry and game as accompaniments. They make stunning salads and even sandwiches. These two berries have been so successfully bred and selected with long seasonal availability and good shelf life that it has become almost the norm to find perfect berries displayed fresh and sparkling on supermarket shelves for months instead of a few frantic weeks. This is an undoubted bonus yet it is not due to limitless technology but more to human ingenuity and passion. The successful strawberry and raspberry story has come about largely because of the co-operation between leading soft fruit suppliers, representing the majority of British growers, National Summer Fruits and selected retailers, in particular

Marks & Spencer are, for most of the year, the country's biggest fresh British raspberry retailer: no surprise there. This company has had a mightily beneficial effect on the world of soft fruit and developments continue at a dizzying pace. Independent and co-operative soft and stone fruit producers are proud of their produce: they want us, the customers, to be more aware of the unique advantages of home-produced British soft and stone fruits, to buy them with real confidence and to consume them with constant pleasure.

MARKS &
SPENCER

Marks & Spencer. Consumers' wishes have been noted. Producers have voiced their concerns and outlined their capabilities to create greater understanding. Specialist fruit breeders have come up with some user-friendly varieties that exceeded all previous expectations.

That it takes 5-10 years to develop a new strawberry variety; that Marks & Spencer strawberries are larger than those of their competitors; that all Marks & Spencer strawberries have been chosen over Spanish, Dutch or Belgian fruit for excellence; that each producer's name stars upon each and every punnet; that one grower has supplied Marks & Spencer for a quarter of a century: and that some fruits come from Ireland, others from East Anglia, Scotland and yet others from Kent, Somerset and Herefordshire may give you some idea of the devotion and commitment that goes into this worthwhile enterprise.

What Are British Summer Fruits?

The term soft fruit often puzzles consumers. Some confuse home-grown produce with imported fruits such as peaches, nectarines, grapes and even melons.

As a practical guide British soft fruits are: strawberries, raspberries, blackberries, red, black and white currants and gooseberries. All these are either grown as plants or on bushes and canes. Plums and cherries are termed stone fruit and are also known as top fruit.

How to select, store and freeze summer fruit.

Always select firm, plump, ripe fruit and eat within two or three days of purchase. It is important that fruit is removed from the fridge and brought to room temperature before eating so that the full flavour can be enjoyed. Freezing both soft and stone fruit enables us to experience the taste of summer all year round and, providing the fruit is fresh, it is easy to prepare and retains its flavour and texture.

STRAWBERRIES

Strawberries were cultivated by the Romans as early as 200 BC. In medieval times strawberries were regarded as an aphrodisiac and soup made of strawberries, borage and soured cream was traditionally served to newly-weds at their wedding breakfast. In the sixteenth century strawberries were sold in cone-shaped straw baskets thus becoming one of the earliest packaged foods. Dr. William Butler originated the famous quotation 'Doubtless God could have made a better berry, but doubtless God never did'.

Nutrition

100 g strawberries (about 10)
27 Kcals
0.0 g fat
2.7 g fibre
77 mg vitamin C (192% RDA)
20 mg folic acid (10% RDA)
0.06 mg vitamin B6 (9% RDA)

They contain more vitamin C than oranges, are high in fibre, low in calories and a good source of folic acid.

Growing

The season begins mid-April with British glasshouse production. The plants are dormant until February when they are 'woken up' and prompted into growth with a little heat and supplementary lighting to fool the plants into thinking they are already into long warm days. By early March the first flowers are emerging and by the second week of April the first fruits can be picked. The peak of production occurs from the end of April until mid-May. The same cycle begins again in late July/early August to enable the fruit to be harvested from mid-September right through until mid-December.

The production of tunnel-protected fruit begins in mid-May and extends to outdoor main crop in June. The process continues and in the autumn strawberries are again protected from bad weather and frosts so that consumers can enjoy British fruit right through until December.

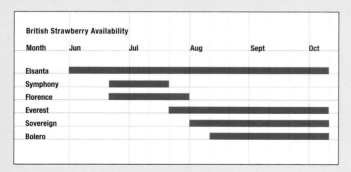

British Strawberry Availability

British Glasshouse Strawberry Availability

Although there are other varieties of strawberry by far the best known and most popular is Elsanta. It has excellent flavour, shelf life and quality and is an attractive glossy berry. Nearly 90% of the fruit found in supermarkets during the main British season will be the Elsanta variety.

RASPBERRIES

Raspberries probably originated in Eastern Asia and it was not until the seventeenth century that the fruit became popular. By the eighteenth century cookery writers were devising recipes using the fruit for raspberry wine and vinegar, sweets and jams. Raspberries were also used as a cure for sore eyes and throats and to cleanse the teeth. Scotland is famous for its raspberry growing and in the late fifties raspberries were taken from Scotland to Covent Garden on a steam train known as the Raspberry Special.

Nutrition

60 g raspberries (about 15 raspberries)
24 Kcals
0.0 g fat
3.8 g fibre
19 mg vitamin C (48% RDA)

High in antioxidant vitamin C and dietary fibre.

Growing

Raspberries are commercially grown for two main markets, the fresh market or for processing. Raspberries were once regarded as a late summer crop but now growers are using varieties and innovative growing methods to extend the season to provide this popular fruit for consumers from mid April through to December. Glasshouse raspberries produce the earliest and latest crops of fruit but no single variety dominates the market since a combination of many varieties allows a consistent supply throughout the season.

CURRANTS

Black, red and white currants were cultivated in the sixteenth century in Holland, Denmark and around the Baltic Sea. During the Second World War there was a big push to grow blackcurrants in this country in order to provide a source of vitamin C that would keep everyone healthy. This led to commercial production that today is mostly used for juice. Red and white currants are eaten fresh but are also used widely as a garnish for both sweet and savoury dishes.

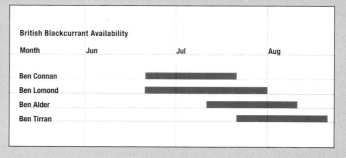

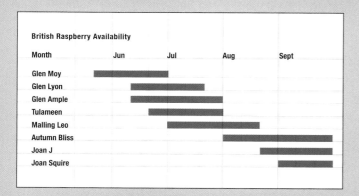

Nutrition

One serving of 100 g blackcurrants

28 Kcals

0.0 g fat

3.6 g fibre (20% RDA)

200 mg vitamin C (500% RDA)

370 mg potassium (10.6% RDA)

1 mg vitamin E (10% RDA)

0.08 mg vitamin B6 (12% RDA)

1.3 mg iron (8.8% RDA)

0.08 mg copper (11.7% RDA)

Weight for weight blackcurrants contain three times as much vitamin C as oranges. They contain useful amounts of vitamin B6, vitamin E, potassium, copper and soluble fibre. They are rich in phytochemicals called anthocyanins.

serving of 100 g redcurrants

21 Kcals

0.0 g fat

3.4 g fibre (19% RDA)

40 mg vitamin C (100% RDA)

1.2 mg iron (8% RDA)

0.12 mg copper (10% RDA)

280 mg potassium (8% RDA)

Rich in vitamin C, useful source of soluble fibre. Contains modest amount of iron, potassium and copper.

Growing

Blackcurrants are primarily grown in the UK for processing into cordials and drinks. Large acreages are grown across the country under contract for blackcurrant drink manufacturers to ensure supply. Blackcurrants are also sold fresh but in limited quantities. Redcurrants are a popular and widely grown currant sold fresh, although consumption on the continent is much higher than in Britain. Whitecurrants can be eaten fresh and

are considered to be the sweetest of the currant family but production and demand in the UK is very small.

BLACKBERRIES

Blackberries grow throughout the world and the fruit has been known in the past by many names, including brambleberries, brumblekites and lawers. There is evidence that blackberries were eaten in Britain in Neolithic times and were surrounded by superstitions. In the south west of England it was believed that the first blackberry spotted growing each year would banish warts. Another tale predicted that blackberries should not be eaten after 10 October because 'during the night the Devil goes by and spits on every bush'.

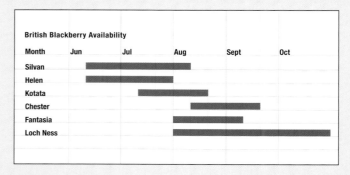

British Blackberry Availability

Nutrition

59 g blackberries (about 10 blackberries)

24 Kcals

0.0 g fat

2.4 g fibre

8 mg vitamin C (19% RDA)

Good source of folate and vitamin E. Studies show that blackberries may reduce the risk of heart disease and inhibit colon cancer.

Growing

There are two distinct types of blackberry, the European and the North American. The North American types tend to fruit earlier in the summer and the combination of the two help to give a consistent supply of blackberries across the season. Most varieties of blackberries have canes that produce thorns, but some of the modern varieties, such as Loch Ness, are thornless.

GOOSEBERRIES

Gooseberries have been grown in Britain since the time of Henry VIII. One ancient belief tells how fairies would shelter from danger in the prickly bushes and hence gooseberries became known as fayberries. Gooseberry juice was also used as a medicine in the treatment of fevers and in the sixteenth century they were recommended to plague victims. In the north of England gooseberry clubs were popular, with members fiercely competing for the varieties that produced the biggest, best and juiciest fruit of the year.

Nutrition

One serving of 100 g raw gooseberries
40 Kcals
0.3 g fat
2.4 g fibre (13% RDA)
26 mg Vitamin C (65% RDA)
Good source of Vitamin C.
Average portion (140 g) stewed gooseberries (without sugar)
22 Kcals
0.4 g fat
2.8 g fibre (15.6% RDA)
15 mg vitamin C (38% RDA)

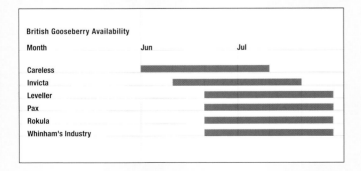

Growing

Gooseberries produce fruits in various colours including green, white and red depending on variety. They are grown on small bushes that are generally spiky and prickly and so can make picking an uncomfortable experience. To make them more manageable some are grown along wires and it is not unusual for bushes to crop for a least twenty years.

PLUMS

Plums grown in Britain originated from fruits of Damascus, Syria and Persia. Plums were brought into this country by a member of the Gage family, hence their link with the gage group of fruits. The famous Victoria Plum was found as a seedling in a garden in Sussex and the Czar was named after a visiting Russian Emperor when the fruit was introduced to the market over one hundred years ago. Plums have stones like human fingerprints, each one being unique to a particular variety. Experts were able to identify over one hundred individual plum stones found on the flagship of Henry VIII's Mary Rose, which sank in 1545 and was raised in the 1980s.

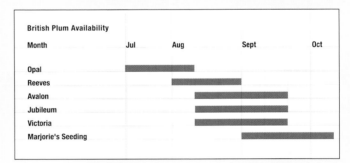

Nutrition

One medium plum
19 Kcals
0.1 g fat
0.8 g fibre
2 mg vitamin C (5% RDA)

Useful source of vitamin A. May reduce risk of colon cancer.

Growing

Due to Britain's difference in climate and season plums have a unique taste that leaves their imported counterpart but a pale imitation. The Victoria plum is the most commonly grown and most popular British variety, but there are many others that are equally deserving of praise. Varieties fall into two main categories, dessert and culinary. Both can be cooked although the culinary varieties with their much sharper taste are usually recommended. A plum orchard would typically crop for twenty years as it takes around five years for the young trees to reach full production.

CHERRIES

The Romans are believed to have discovered sweet cherries in Asia Minor in about 70 BC and introduced them to Britain in the first century AD. Although the fruit has always been popular for dessert and culinary purposes, cherries were used during the fifteenth and sixteenth centuries for their medicinal properties. The German word Kirsch, the cherry liqueur, came from the word *karshu*, the name given to the first cultivated cherries in Mesopotamia in 8 BC. Hot cherry stones were once used in bed-warming pans and Shakespeare's *A Midsummer Night's Dream* associates cherries with love and romance.

Nutrition

100 g cherries (about 10 cherries)

48 Kcals

0.1 g fat

2.1 g fibre

11 mg vitamin C (27% RDA)

Rich in bioflavonoids and ellagic acid. Studies show cherries to be a good source of antioxidants and darker cherries will have higher levels than red/yellow ones.

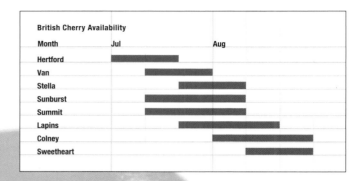

British Cherry Availability

Month	Jul	Aug
Hertford		
Van		
Stella		
Sunburst		
Summit		
Lapins		
Colney		
Sweetheart		

Growing

In the past cherry trees were very large, up to forty feet high and with similar spread. Although the trees looked magnificent they became increasingly difficult to manage. Since the mid seventies the tree size has been slowly reduced and today the cherry industry is entering a new phase, with smaller trees and new varieties that are easy to pick. Growers have renewed confidence to invest in many new orchards and it is hoped as these orchards come into full bearing, that consumer sales of this popular fruit will continue to increase.

strawberries

STRAWBERRIES are delicious eaten raw, or with sugar and cream and even with a dash of black pepper. They provide the basis for an endless supply of dessert recipes from popular tarts, mousses and homemade ice cream to special treats such as strawberries served steeped in champagne. Strawberry jam is a firm favourite and pureed fruit can make a delicious drink or be used to complement main course dishes.

Try these easy, elegant open sandwiches as snacks with some chilled beer, an iced rosé wine or perhaps with long drinks of iced tea. Alternatively make mini versions on crisp cracker biscuits as cocktail snacks for a party.

strawberry, parma ham and mint open sandwiches

Slice the ciabatta lengthways into two flat portions. Halve each one crosswise, to make 4 portions. Toast the cut surfaces briefly or leave untoasted. Using the cheese, spread some on each piece. Twist a slice of ham on to each. Use the strawberries to cover the sandwiches prettily. Grind salt and pepper over all. Whisk together the oil and the two vinegars and the chopped mint. Drizzle some over each sandwich. Garnish using the remaining sprigs and serve with appropriate drinks.

Tip: Other breads such as pane integrate, focaccia or even rye bread or pumpernickel could be substituted, but they must be dense enough to support the topping easily, and the flavour should not overwhelm the fruit.

1 ciabatta loaf
200 g cream cheese, quark or cheese spread
8 slices parma ham or jamon serrano (cured ham)
200 g fresh, ripe strawberries, hulled, halved lengthways
Vinaigrette:
2 tbsp extra virgin olive oil
1 tbsp red wine vinegar
1 tsp balsamic vinegar
10 g fresh mint sprigs, chopped (reserve 8 sprigs as garnish)

Serves 4

Victorian and Edwardian recipe books often feature fresh fruit cordials. Modern versions have many uses. Refrigerated, this recipe will keep for four weeks. Use it as the basis for alcoholic cocktails, for simple fruit drinks with soda and ice; with ice creams as a sauce; over fresh berries themselves as glaze, and fold it into ricotta, curd or cream cheese or mascarpone for an almost instant dessert, accompanied by extra fresh berries and crisp wafers. Divine!

summer strawberry cordial

250 g fresh, very ripe, strawberries, hulled, finely chopped
100 g caster sugar
100 ml water
1 tsp tartaric acid (or 2 tbsp fresh lemon juice)
12 ice cubes, crushed
4 tbsp gin or white rum (optional)
4 tbsp fruit brandy; eau-de-vie de fraise or other schnapps of choice (optional)

Makes 500 ml (enough for 20 servings)

Put the berries into a blender. Heat the sugar and water with the tartaric acid, until very hot then pour this into the blender and blend, on full power for 1 minute until evenly smooth. Now add the ice, and the two kinds of liquor (if using). Whiz again to make a gorgeous pink syrup. Strain through a plastic or stainless steel sieve to remove the seeds. Pour into a hot, sterilized bottle and allow to cool, then cork or screw on the top. Refrigerate. Use within 6 weeks. To use as a drink: add 2 tablespoons of cordial, some ice, and the mixer of your choice: soda, tonic, dry sparkling wine or even gin or rum.

Note: If not fortified with alcohol, use this recipe within 1 week.

Baked cheesecake is often of German or Alsace origin: this version contains strawberry chunks and is topped with a fresh strawberry puree-cum-compote: a delicious finishing touch, instead of the usual jam or jelly glaze.

strawberry cheesecake with a red compote glaze

Preheat the oven to 180°C, 350°F, Gas 4. Butter the inside of the cake tin. In a large bowl whisk the vanilla sugar, cream cheese and cornflour together until very smooth: about 2-3 minutes using an electric whisk, rotary beater or balloon whisk. Beat in the eggs, one at a time, scraping the sides down now and then using a rubber spatula. Add the lemon juice, salt and sour cream and beat well until fully blended. Now scatter 16 berry halves over the base of the tin. Pour the mix into the prepared cake tin. Set cake tin on baking tray and place in the oven. Bake the cake towards the bottom of the oven for 1 hour until barely firm to the touch at the centre. Turn off the oven but leave the door closed. Leave undisturbed for 45 minutes. Remove the cake tin to a wire rack. Leave it to cool to room temperature: this takes about an hour.

Now cook the remaining fresh strawberries (keeping about a fifth for decoration). Using a potato masher crush them with the sugar over heat for about 5 minutes, until bubbling and thick. Add a few drops of lemon juice. Turn off the heat and cool the compote over chilled water. To serve the cake, run a knife blade around the edge of the cake. Loosen and remove the tin. Slide a knife between the cheesecake and the base of the cake tin. Slide the cake onto a serving dish. Pour some cool compote on top allowing some to trickle down the sides. Serve extra compote in a bowl with the cake. Decorate the top with halved berries. Dust with icing sugar.

Serve as a classic dessert or with tea or with coffee.

200 g vanilla sugar or caster sugar

450 g full fat soft cheese (e.g Philadelphia)

1 tbsp cornflour

3 medium eggs

3 tbsp freshly squeezed lemon juice

$\frac{1}{4}$ tsp salt

725 ml sour cream

400 g fresh strawberries, hulled and halved

100 g caster sugar

2 tsp fresh lemon juice

icing sugar for dusting

butter (to grease the cake tin)

20.5 cm diameter loose-bottomed, spring form cake tin

1 large baking tray or sheet

foil (for wrapping the cake tin)

Serves 8

Strawberries, sharp, sweet and scented, combine perfectly with fresh herbs and several other aromatics to make a sensational salsa: a lean, uncooked sauce, which can be hand-chopped or made using a food processor. It tastes especially good with ham, pork or gammon but complements oily fish such as salmon and tuna, as well.

strawberry and chilli salsa

Halve the strawberries and set them flat on a chopping board. Use a sharp knife, cleaver or mezzaluna to chop them finely. Pile them into a bowl adding the orange juice and zest, chopped onion, chilli, the garlic, salt and vinegar and stir well until mixed. Leave for 5-10 minutes. Stir in the herbs and serve. Alternatively put all of the prepared ingredients into a food processor and process, in bursts, to a rough mix: but not a puree. (Not as pretty, but delicious.)

Uses: Spoon over roast pork, with griddled gammon steaks, or with ham salad. Serve instead of apple sauce with smoked mackerel, beside some griddled salmon, on tuna steaks or with fish cakes.

250 g fresh strawberries, hulled

1 fresh orange, juice squeezed, zest shredded

1 small red onion, chopped finely

2 fresh red or green chillies, deseeded, membranes removed, sliced finely

2 garlic cloves, crushed

2 tsp sea salt flakes

2 tbsp fruit vinegar such as raspberry or blackcurrant

10 g fresh mint, tarragon, basil, lovage or celery leaves, scissor-snipped

Makes 400 ml

A pudding which is one of the joys of summer. This famous recipe is superb and yet amazingly simple to make. It is best made a day in advance. Use four individual cups, ramekins, small bowls or even wine glasses of 200 ml volume as the containers. Chilled overnight the pudding will turn out in neat little shapes – beautiful as well as delicious.

strawberry brioche pudding

Put half of the crushed fruit into a food processor. Boil the vanilla sugar and water together briefly, to make a syrup. Pour this into the fruit. Blitz for about 20 seconds to give a gorgeous, messy, red puree. Pour this out into a shallow bowl. Slice the brioche into slices about 6 mm thick then cut into fingers of suitable size to line the sides of the ramekins (about 200 ml volume each). Line each ramekin with enough cling film to have some overhanging. Dip the brioche fingers quickly into the puree. Overlap them so that they line the containers. Spoon some of the crushed mixed fruit into each. Add more fruit-soaked brioche fingers and spoon in more berries. Continue in layers until all the fruit, the puree and most, or all, of the brioche has been used up. If necessary, crush or crumble the last few pieces of bread to get a neat fit. Cover the puddings with the excess cling film, folding it over the top. Set weights on top (tumblers filled with water are an easy solution). Chill for 12 to 24 hours (you cannot guarantee a firm shape unless this time is allowed). Turn out just before serving by unwrapping and pulling on the cling film: the pudding comes out perfectly. Dust with some icing sugar if you like and a few extra berries, maybe. Have available some thin cream for diners to help themselves. Decorate prettily: this is a celebration dessert and a real treat.

Tip: Brioche is sweetened, egg-enriched bread dough. If no brioche can be found, use a good, soft, slightly sweet white bread, instead, or even soft, plain sponge cake.

225 g fresh strawberries, hulled, quartered, crushed

225 g fresh raspberries, crushed

170 g fresh red currants, stemmed, crushed

100 g vanilla sugar

150 ml boiling water

1 long brioche loaf, about 400g (from good bakers or certain supermarkets)

To serve:

icing sugar, sieved, for dusting (optional)

300 ml thin cream (optional)

Serves 4

These luscious little desserts seem to capture the essence of summer's sweet scentedness. The individual jellies, of real puree, are cloudy pink and very special. They have just enough gelatine to set them softly: turning them out is not always successful but for a firmer set, to allow you to turn them out, you can increase the quantity of gelatine. For luxurious summer picnics, set the jellies in clear plastic tumblers or goblets: they travel well, if kept cool.

luxury strawberry champagne jellies

Put three-quarters of the strawberries, with the boiling water and sugar into a food processor or blender. Blitz for 30 seconds or so. Set this mixture in a nylon or stainless steel sieve set over a bowl. Leave this to drip: this will take about 2 hours. Meanwhile soften the gelatine in 200 ml of the wine (if a firmer jelly is required use twice the amount of gelatine). Heat over boiling water (or in a microwave for 30-second bursts) until completely dissolved. Cool. Stir in the liqueur. Measure the strawberry liquid (there should be at least 600 ml). Stir this in and the rest of the champagne. Leave to cool. Meanwhile arrange the remaining fruits of choice into the base of 4, 6 or 8 serving goblets, tumblers or glass dessert dishes. Spoon over the slightly setting jelly. Chill for 4-5 hours if possible or until set. Eat directly from the glasses.

450 g ripe, fresh strawberries, hulled
300 ml boiling water
150 g caster sugar
2 sachets granulated gelatine (about 1 tsp each sachet)
500 ml sweet champagne
100 ml cointreau or curaçao liqueur
To decorate:
100 g - 200 g sliced fresh strawberries, red currants, raspberries or a mix

Serves 4, 6 or 8 depending on size of container

Note: Use the unstrained berry puree left in the sieve as flavouring for yogurt or stirred into custard. It is utterly delicious and far too good to discard. Alternatively spread it on hot buttered toast, for breakfast.

Gorgeous colour, superb flavour and delectable jelly-like, soft texture makes this recipe truly special. Make a few small pots as treats whenever really good fresh berries are available. Use this jam within 1 month: no difficulty there. It is great for cream teas: on toasted bread or crumpets, in sponge cakes, to stir into natural yogurt and to top a cheesecake or even inside muffins. Use small pots, beautifully labelled and wrapped, as gifts for friends.

sensational strawberry jam

900 g fresh, perfect strawberries
675 g caster sugar
1 tbsp ascorbic acid (vitamin C) powder, tartaric or citric acid crystals
1 tbsp butter
4 x 225 g (or 8 x 125 g) clean, sterilized jars, with lids or cellophane covers, rubber bands and waxed paper discs

Makes 1 kg (about 4 pots or jars)

Hull and halve the berries and put into a large, clean, heavy-based saucepan or preserving pan. Add half of the sugar. Using a potato masher, crush up and mash some of the berries with the sugar. Leave for several hours, or overnight if you prefer, then add the remaining sugar. Bring the pan contents to simmering, then to a rapid boil. Cook stirring occasionally for 10 minutes. Sprinkle in the ascorbic acid: the jam will turn a superb scarlet. Stir well. Remove from the heat. Test a spoonful on a cold saucer: it should form a slight skin. Add the knob of butter, stirring gently to help reduce any foam. Stand the clean hot jars on a board or cloth. Pour the hot jam into the jars, using a jam funnel or jug, distributing the fruit as evenly as possible. Cool. Cover each pot with a wax paper disc. Once jam is cold, screw on sterilized lids. Alternatively, cover with wetted, stretched cellophane covers. Secure with rubber bands. Cover, seal and label. Store in a cool dark place. Use within 1 month for maximum flavour.

Note: To sterilize jars pour 60 ml (4 tbsp) hot water into each jar. Microwave on HIGH for 1½ minutes or until boiling, using oven gloves to pour out the water. Invert the jars onto clean kitchen paper or a sterile wire rack. The hot jars are ready for use. Or using a conventional oven, wash jars in very hot water, dry thoroughly, then warm in the oven on a very low setting, ideally on a baking tray padded with paper, to stop them cracking.

Buy the vitamin C powder from your chemist. Tartaric or citric acids are other useful alternatives, from grocers.

raspberries

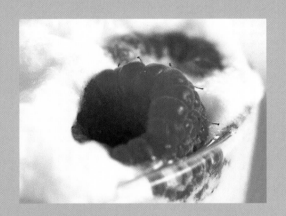

RASPBERRIES are the second most popular fruit to strawberries. They are the most versatile of all British fruits and their superb flavour makes them a favourite eaten raw or made into a multitude of desserts, with their rich colour giving a wonderful eye-catching appeal that cannot be resisted. They are excellent for freezing or making into ice cream and can even be used to flavour vinegar for an unusual salad dressing.

An unusual raspberry-mustard vinaigrette helps to glaze these chicken breasts. More is trickled over the salad at serving time. You can sieve out the seeds or leave them in: it's up to you. But the freshness of red berries is the outrageously fresh detail that sets this recipe apart.

chicken breasts with raspberry vinaigrette on baby salad leaves

Preheat the oven to 180°C, 350°F, Gas 4. Lightly rub the chicken pieces with a little of the oil and set, evenly spaced, on a baking tray. Slash each breast twice on the diagonal. Combine the remaining oil with the other 6 ingredients in a blender. Blitz continuously for 30 seconds to make the vinaigrette. Sieve it or leave it as it is. Spoon about 2 tablespoons of vinaigrette over each chicken piece. Bake for 25-30 minutes, spooning some more berry vinaigrette over, after 20 minutes of cooking. Test one chicken breast with a skewer or fork to check doneness, it should be firm and white right through. Slice the breasts crosswise into bite-sized pieces. Spoon some extra vinaigrette on or around them, and add some baby salad leaves to complete the dish. Serve with crusty bread and perhaps some potato, pasta or rice salad, to make a balanced main course meal. Serve hot, warm or cool.

Tips:
- Serve the chicken cold, on cocktail sticks, as a snack.
- Fill a split pitta bread with the salad, add the chicken pieces and vinaigrette and eat as a picnic lunch.
- Toss the chicken and its sauce through some couscous for an unusual salad: very handsome if also garnished with radicchio and lollo rosso leaves.
- Add some chilli paste or Thai red curry paste to the vinaigrette and garnish the dish using red basil for a really exotic effect.

4 large (about 150 g each) skinned, boned chicken breasts

2 tbsp extra virgin olive oil

170 g fresh raspberries

2 tbsp coarse grain mustard

1 tbsp light soy sauce

2 tbsp fruit vinegar such as raspberry vinegar

2 garlic cloves, chopped finely

2 shallots or 1 small onion, chopped finely

100 g mixed baby leaf salad of choice, to serve

Serves 4

A funky summer drink using fresh summer berries and ice cream. Fun for the whole family to make and easy too, but stylish.

raspberry floats

Put a quarter of the raspberries into each of 4 tall tumblers, chilled if possible. Add the caster sugar. Use the handle of a wooden spoon or a honey trickler to mash the berries and sugar to a gorgeous red mush. Some may remain whole. Now pour some orange juice into each glass. Add two scoops of ice cream to each (or cut it up into 8 even cubes to save time). Now push a spoon down the side of each glass. Trickle in chilled soft drink and let it fizz up and mix. Serve with two wide straws. Drink without delay.

Note: For a more adult version you could use tonic, not soda, and add 2 tablespoons of fruit brandy (schnapps) or cognac to each drink before topping up.

170 g fresh raspberries (or defrosted raspberries)

4 tsp caster sugar

100 ml freshly squeezed orange juice or raspberry-orange juice

600 ml vanilla ice cream

600 ml ice cream soda, 7-Up or lemonade, chilled

Serves 4

This classic college pudding is really a fruit, cream and meringue mixture: a perfect blend of glorious colours, textures and tastes.

raspberry and strawberry meringue fool

If using bought meringues, simply crush them into bite-sized bits. To make your own meringues, combine the ingredients, in the order given in a heat-proof bowl which is standing in 2 cm of near-boiling water. Using an electric whisk, whisk the mixture continuously until it forms a dense, glossy meringue, which holds its shape. Wet some sheets of silicone/ non-stick/ bakewell paper and cover 2 baking trays with them. Fill a piping bag or use two teaspoons and shape 60-80 small meringues, evenly spaced on the trays. Bake in the oven pre-heated to 140°C/ 275°F/ Gas 1 for 1 1/4 hours. Use 100 g weight of these meringues for this recipe. (Use remaining meringues for later desserts.) Crush them roughly.

For the pudding: roughly mash the berries and most of the icing sugar and fold in some smashed meringues. First spoon this, then some cream into goblets, bowls or even tumblers, repeating the process until all the ingredients are used. Refrigerate until ready to serve. Then sprinkle some icing sugar on top before serving.

150 g fresh raspberries

100 g fresh strawberries, hulled (very ripe if possible)

25 g icing sugar

200 ml double cream, whipped

100 g meringues, bought or home-made (see recipe below)

Never-Fail Meringues

325 g caster sugar

2 egg whites

1 tsp malt vinegar

1/2 tsp almond essence

4 tbsp boiling water

Serves 4 - 6

Not only is there a tint of raspberry in the custard but there are raspberries on top and a wonderful crisp crust of caramel. Superb! A perfect party dessert.

raspberry brûlée

Preheat the oven to 110°C, 225°F, Gas ¼. Have ready four heatproof china, metal or glass ramekins, each about 150 ml volume. Put the cream, vanilla pod and milk into a pan. Bring to boiling point. Remove the pan from the heat.

Remove and drain the vanilla pod. Use a knife to scrape out and add the sticky black seeds to the custard. Whisk them in. Now put the yolks into a heatproof bowl. Whisk them with two-thirds of the sugar until pale. Pour the cream and milk mixture on to the yolks, stir until all the sugar is evenly dissolved. Pour the custard, through a fine sieve, into the four ramekins, also adding 8 raspberries, which have been mashed with a little of the reserved sugar. Bake the rosy custards for 1-1¼ hours or until set but still wobbly.

Remove from the oven. Cool quickly by placing ramekins in iced water then chill for 2 hours. Now arrange some of the remaining raspberries on top of each custard. In a dry, clean heavy frypan, heat the remaining sugar (about 40 g) over high heat, about 2-3 minutes, shaking the pan but never stirring it. Once the sugar has caramelized to mid-brown (deep brown means it will taste burned) drizzle it over the berry-decorated custards. Serve within an hour, while the caramel is crispy.

200 ml double cream

1 vanilla pod, slit lengthways

150 ml creamy (whole) milk

6 medium egg yolks

175 g caster sugar

170 g fresh raspberries

Serves 4

This fresh, uncooked fruit sauce must be one of the most famous ever invented. It works its intense, vivid, sweet-sharp magic on whatever you pair it with. Enjoy a little dish of it alone or with a few whole berries – it is bliss!

crimson raspberry coulis

Using a food processor, whiz all the ingredients to a smooth, crimson puree in a continuous burst. Push the sauce through a nylon or stainless steel sieve (other metal sieves can give a metallic taste), it makes about 425 ml of finished sauce. Store in a covered container in the fridge. Use within 4 days in any one of the following ways:

- Serve with berries, scoops of vanilla ice cream and crisp wafer biscuits.
- Serve with cream-topped Pavlova or individual meringues and fresh strawberries, or blackberries or a mixture.
- Serve with brandy snaps piped full of sweetened mascarpone.
- Use to decorate a tropical fruit salad: drizzle the coulis over chunks of mango, melon, pineapple and grapes.
- Serve the coulis around some poached pear halves that have been filled with crushed amaretti biscuits, scoops of chocolate ganache or ice cream. Gorgeous!
- Set the coulis, using gelatine dissolved in a little sweet wine (allow one sachet per 300 ml coulis) to make an impressively rich, dense fruit jelly.
- Add some balsamic vinegar (2 tablespoons per 300 ml) and serve with roast duck, goose or venison as a savoury sauce.
- Serve with bran flakes and thick Greek yogurt for a breakfast in a million.

340 g (2 punnets) fresh raspberries

1 cup icing sugar (about 125 g)

3 tbsp fresh lemon juice

3 tbsp dark rum, cognac or armagnac

Makes 425 ml

currants

BLACKCURRANT compote sweetened with honey or sugar served with cinnamon ice cream is very special. Blackcurrants also make perfect jam because they are high in pectin content. They freeze well and also give a lovely flavour to pies and crumbles when combined with other fruits.

An effortless and luxurious way to serve lean, succulent lamb. Fresh redcurrants are crushed into the sauce and extra ones are used as a beautiful, edible garnish. Chining the lamb racks means that the bones are easy to carve at the table. Make this when young lamb is available and redcurrants are at their peak.

redcurrants with rosy rack of lamb

2 x 7 or 8 bone racks of lamb (about 800 g total), all fat removed, frenched and chined (ask your butcher to do this)

2 tsp dark soy sauce

2 garlic cloves, crushed

1 tbsp Dijon-style mustard

1 tbsp anchovy paste or 4 canned anchovies, mashed to a puree

1 tsp clear honey

170 g fresh redcurrants

2 tbsp redcurrant jelly or other red berry jelly

6 tbsp rosé or red wine

Freshly ground black pepper

Serves 4

Preheat the oven to 200°C, 400°F, Gas 6. Pat dry the two prepared racks of lean, lamb cutlets using kitchen paper. Mix together the soy, garlic, mustard and anchovy and use this paste to rub over all surfaces of the meat. Wrap the long bones in foil to cover them. Set the coated lamb, (foil-covered bones upwards), propped against each other, in a small, shallow roasting pan. Roast for 20-25 minutes or until the meat is firm but still rosy inside, when tested. Remove the lamb from the oven. Cover it. Leave it to rest while you make the sauce. Keep at least 4 whole strings of the redcurrants for garnish. Pull the remaining currants off their stems and add them to the roasting pan. Heat the pan contents, mashing in the currants and cooking them with the pan sediment and the red berry jelly, over a moderate heat, until the gravy bubbles up and thickens. Add the wine. Stir again over moderate heat to make a thin fruity gravy. Taste and season with black pepper. Pour into a jug or sauce boat. Serve 3-4 cutlets of lamb per person, one gorgeous string of currants and a pool of sauce per person, with vegetables of your own choice.

Tip: Separated and served cold, these lamb cutlets and their sauce make perfect picnic food, for young and old, and also excellent buffet snacks.

A beautiful, sharp, fragrant dessert to make and serve whenever currants are available. Because the flavour is so intense, only a small portion is needed per serving, though some people may like second helpings.

blackcurrant sorbet

Have a sorbetiere or ice-cream maker ready and cold. Combine the currants with the sugar in a blender. Pour in the boiling water and the lemon juice. Blitz continuously for about 45 seconds, until they are a deep purple red puree. Strain this puree through a nylon or stainless steel sieve (an ordinary metal sieve may taint the flavour.) Measure the volume: there should be about 1 litre. Cool then chill the puree then whisk in the egg white. Pour into the sorbetiere and churn according to the manufacturer's instructions, until the sorbet is set, firm but still creamy. Use immediately or pack into a freezer container (about 1 litre volume), cover, label and freeze until time of use.

To make without an ice-cream maker: do not add the egg white at the start. Freeze the fruit mixture in a shallow 1 litre freezer container for 1½-2 hours or until crystals have formed at the edges. Turn mixture out into a bowl and add the whisked egg white. Whisk to mix using a balloon whisk. Return to container and refreeze. Repeat this whisking process twice more.

Whichever method you use to make sorbet let it "condition" for 30-40 minutes in the fridge before you serve it. Serve the sorbet in scoops in goblets, or dishes with some trickles of cassis, if liked, over the top. Serve with optional crisp wafers.

Tip: Though this can be frozen for weeks or even months, I feel it is best used within a few days.

3 x 170 g punnets blackcurrants, stems removed

150 g caster sugar

250 ml boiling water

3 tbsp lemon juice

1 egg white, whisked to a foam

To serve:

4 tbsp crème de cassis (optional)

4 crisp wafer biscuits (optional)

Serves 4-6

blackberries

BLACKBERRIES are rich and juicy and perfect companions for game and apples. Their dark colour and distinctive flavour combines to make wonderful jams, jellies and sauces and they also freeze well. Cooked blackberries, slightly sweetened, scattered over a pancake that has a dash of gin added to the mixture and dusted with icing sugar, are delicious.

What bliss: fruity muffins filled with blackberries and a hint of nut. Enjoy these easy treats whenever you find some plump, glossy blackberries in the farmers' market, fruit shop or your local supermarket. Serve for breakfast, with afternoon tea or as a lunch box treat.

blackberry, orange and nut muffins

Preheat the oven to 200°C, 400°F, Gas 6. Brush the inside of each paper case with a little oil. Set on a baking tray. Or prepare muffin tin. Melt the butter and stir in the nuts. Sift together the flour, baking powder, baking soda and sugar into a large mixing bowl. Combine the zest, juice, milk and egg. Whisk together briefly then stir in the butter and nut mixture. Pour the liquid ingredients into a well in the dry ingredients, quickly mixing with a fork until you get a rough, uneven, bubbly mix (do not over mix: you do not want a smooth muffin mixture). Toss in some of the berries. Now use two dessert spoons to spoon the soft muffin mix evenly into the paper cases. Push the rest of the berries on top. Bake for 18-22 minutes or until risen, crusty and damp but set in the centre, if broken open. Serve warm, dusted with a little icing sugar and with a sliver of chilled butter inside.

Muffin tin or 8 or 12-paper muffin cases

1 tbsp olive oil (to brush muffin cases)

75 g butter

50 g finely chopped hazelnuts

250 g plain flour

1 tsp baking powder

¼ tsp baking soda

75 g caster sugar

zest of 1 orange, in fine shreds or grated

100 ml freshly squeezed orange juice

100 ml creamy (whole) milk

1 egg

170 g fresh blackberries

Makes 8 or 12 medium muffins

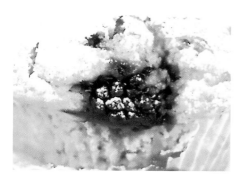

Here's a teenager's dream breakfast, an adult's health food treat and a cool dessert all in one: a beautiful berry smoothie. Its colour is a ravishing deep purple. Serve it in glasses or in goblets.

blackberry "blush" smoothie

Combine 300 g of the blackberries, half of the honey and all of the orange juice in a blender. Whiz to a puree. Add the banana, the yogurt and the ice cubes. Blitz again to make a rosy drink. Now combine the remaining berries and the remaining honey. Mash them to a crush using a fork. Spoon some of this into the base of each serving tumbler with a little of the extra yogurt. Pour some smoothie into each of the glasses, topping up with more yogurt if liked. Serve with thick straws and a long spoon to spoon up the berries at the base.

4 tall tumblers, to serve

450 g fresh blackberries

2 tbsp clear honey

250 ml freshly squeezed orange juice

I banana, skinned and chopped

350 ml natural yogurt plus extra for serving

8 ice cubes

Serves 4 (makes I litre)

A Yorkshire pudding tray with four large, shallow holes or four individual Yorkshire pudding baking tins of about 7.5 cm diameter are perfect for this. Cream and/or custard are superbly suitable accompaniments, or thick yogurt. A gloriously luscious confection, based on the famous French dessert made using apples.

blackberry tartes tatin

Preheat the oven to 200°C, 400°F, Gas 6. Divide the berries between a lightly buttered 4 × bun tin or Yorkshire pudding baking tins. Stir the butter and sugar together over heat, with a squeeze of lemon juice, stirring until a fragrant, hot, bubbling butterscotch mixture forms. Pour this equally over the berries. Set the tin or pans in the hot oven.

Now quickly mix the butter, icing sugar, egg, flour and cinnamon together to make a soft pastry. Divide it into four. Pat and roll each ball out to give four discs about 7.5 cm across.

Remove tins from the oven and drop one pastry disc on the top of each of the hot berry portions, pushing pastry well down. Bake undisturbed for 15-20 minutes or until the pastry is set. Remove from the oven. Leave to stand for 1 minute. Cover each tarte tatin with a flat plate. (If using a four-hole pudding tray invert onto a large platter.) Invert each pudding, tipping out each tatin and its juices. Serve hot with ice cream and pouring custard if liked.

Berry Base:
340 g fresh blackberries
50 g butter, melted
50 g light brown muscovado sugar
1 tbsp lemon juice

Pastry Topping:
50 g softened butter
45 g icing sugar
1 egg beaten
125 g plain flour
1 tsp powdered cinnamon

Serves 4

This chocolate cake is based on an Austrian recipe: it contains no flour and is rich, dark and dense, almost like a mousse. Some blackberries are cooked within it; the remainder are mashed up with eau-de-vie, sugar and cream to make a "fool" which is also an accompanying sauce: absolutely delicious, though you could simply substitute cream, and enjoy the berries whole.

chocolate and blackberry torte with blackberry fool sauce

Preheat the oven to 180°C, 350°F, Gas 4 . Grease a 23 cm loose-based cake tin and line the base with baking parchment. Cut the butter into cubes and break up the chocolate. Put the butter and chocolate in a bowl and melt in the microwave on HIGH for 1-1 ½ minutes or set the bowl over a pan of boiling water (do not allow bowl to touch the water) and stir until melted, smooth and glossy. Separate the eggs, then stir the yolks into the chocolate mixture. Add the ground hazelnuts and stir lightly until evenly mixed. Whisk the egg whites using an electric whisk until peaks form. Add the sugar in 2 lots and continue beating until stiff peaks form, about 3-4 minutes. Fold a quarter into the chocolate mixture. When this is evenly mixed fold in another quarter, then the remaining egg white mixture. Turn into the prepared tin and shake the tin to level the mixture. Place half the berries evenly on top of the cake mixture. Bake for 35-45 minutes until firm to touch and a skewer inserted into the centre comes out clean. Leave in the tin to cool for 1 hour. Meanwhile mash the remaining berries and the vanilla sugar in a small bowl. Stir through the schnapps and crème fraîche. Refrigerate until serving. You can dust the torte with stripes of sieved icing sugar and sieved cocoa in a pattern to finish off if you like. Serve cut into 8 or 12 wedges. Add a dollop of the blackberry fool sauce, as a bonus.

Note: This cake can be made 1, 2 or 3 days ahead, wrapped and chilled (or frozen) and then used when convenient. It is a party giver's delight. It even survives being frozen.

Torte:

100 g butter

150 g plain chocolate

5 eggs

150 g ground hazelnuts

100 g light muscovado sugar

170 g fresh blackberries (reserving half for the fool)

Fool:

2 tbsp vanilla sugar

1 tsp fruit schnapps e.g. apricot or raspberry

500 g crème fraîche

To decorate: sieved icing sugar and sieved cocoa powder (optional)

Serves 8-12

gooseberries

BRITISH GOOSEBERRIES have a characteristically sharp taste that can make an ordinary dish into something special. Whilst traditional gooseberry fools and pies are still very popular, gooseberries also make excellent jams, crumbles, and delicious wine and can be used as an accompaniment to meat and fish. The combination of gooseberries and elderflower really has an exquisite flavour when made into a puree or sorbet.

This colourful, lively uncooked sauce is perfect served with sausages, smoked mackerel, smoked salmon, roast poultry, game, with gammon or ham. It also complements cheese: try an open cheddar cheese sandwich with this salsa instead of the more traditional chutney.

gooseberry salsa

Top and tail the gooseberries and chop roughly. Whiz them briefly in one burst, in a food processor with the lime juice, olive oil, honey and soy sauce until a rough puree results. Stir in the lime zest, then add the ginger, spring onions, garlic, chilli and coriander, and stir again. Taste. Adjust seasonings and serve with the protein food of your choice.

170 g fresh gooseberries

1 fresh lime; zest shredded, juice squeezed

2 tbsp extra virgin olive oil

2 tbsp clear honey (or more)

1 tbsp light soy sauce

2.5 cm piece fresh ginger, peeled, shredded

4 spring onions, finely sliced

2 garlic cloves, finely chopped

1/2 fresh green chilli (bird's eye or serrano)

20 g fresh coriander leaves, scissor-chopped

freshly ground black pepper and sea salt

Makes 275 ml

Tips:

- If no fresh green chilli is available, substitute 1/2 teaspoon hot chilli sauce; or 1-2 tablespoons freshly grated horseradish, or some Japanese wasabi paste (about 1/2-1 teaspoonful).
- Refrigerated, the salsa keeps well for 2 days but may need some fresh herbs to be added, to refresh the colour.

This must be one of the simplest, but most popular desserts ever dreamed up. Even using frozen or canned gooseberries it tastes delicious.

gooseberry and elderflower fool

Top and tail the fresh gooseberries. Prick them once using a fork. Put them into a large lidded saucepan with half of the sugar and all of the elderflower cordial. Cook, shaking the covered pan, over gentle heat for 12-15 minutes or until they are barely soft. Leave them to cool. Drain off, into a food processor, about 125 ml of the syrupy juices which form, with half of the drained, cooked, cooled gooseberries. Whiz to a rough puree. Fold this into the thick custard. Fold this into the yogurt. Now divide the reserved gooseberries and their juices between four or six goblets, tumblers or small serving bowls. Spoon the gooseberry custard and yogurt fool into each. Continue until all the mixture is used up. Chill. Serve straight away or within 24 hours.

Note: You can add 1 sachet of gelatine to some of the gooseberry syrup. Leave to swell. Microwave until melted then fold into the dessert: a denser, firmer mixture is achieved.

340 g fresh gooseberries

100 g caster sugar

6 tbsp elderflower cordial

200 g ready-made vanilla pouring custard

500 g strained thick Greek yoghurt

Serves 4-6

plums

PLUMS are one of the glory fruits of Britain with many distinctive flavours. Different dessert and culinary varieties mean traditional comfort food such as plum crumble and pie can be eaten alongside amazing ice cream and unusual sauces to accompany savoury dishes. They also freeze well and make delicious chutneys and wine.

A classic but absolutely invaluable jam, good for many uses in the kitchen. All plums are suitable but red-fleshed ones give a particularly superb colour.

plum and cinnamon jam

Combine the plums, sugar and juice and bring to a boil, stirring, until the sugar is dissolved. Add the cinnamon and allspice. Cook, uncovered, at a gentle, steady simmer for 12-15 minutes or until a spoonful, on a chilled plate, forms a skin when pushed with a finger. Leave to cool, gently stirring in the butter, if liked. Pour into 3 or 4 hot sterilized pots or jars. Leave to cool then cover each pot with a waxed paper disc. Screw on a lid or use wetted, stretched cellophane and rubber bands. Label and store in a cool dark place. Use within 6 months.

Use as:

- a topping for toasted, buttered bread, buttered teacakes, crumpets or on buns.
- on top of dropped scones, crumpets, pikelets and scones.
- on natural yogurt and cereal for breakfast.
- with sliced bananas and yogurt, as a dessert.
- mixed with a little lemon juice, lime juice or vinegar as a glaze for roasts, grills or kebabs.

1 kg fresh ripe soft plums, halved, stones removed

600 g granulated sugar (or jam sugar, containing pectin)

150 ml fresh orange juice

6 sticks cinnamon, broken into halves

2 tbsp ground allspice

1 tbsp butter (optional)

Makes 3 or 4 medium pots or jars

A delicious Asian-spiced, chutney-like, long-keeping sauce. Use with oriental dishes, kebabs, rice and noodles, also with duck or game. Poultry, also fish and chips can benefit from its charms: they seem more sophisticated in its company. Bread and cheese, with some of this plum sauce, becomes a feast. It is a wonderfully versatile recipe.

spicy savoury plum sauce

Simmer the plums, onions, garlic, ginger and tea in a large uncovered pan for 15 minutes or until softened and most of the liquid has evaporated. Add the vinegar, cinnamon, spice, chillies and sugar, turn up the heat and stir until dissolved. Be careful as it will bubble and splatter. Bring to the boil and cook uncovered for 15 minutes or until the sauce is thick. Once a spoonful, if put onto a saucer forms a skin, it is ready. Let the sauce cool. Put into a blender (for a smoother effect) or food processor (rougher texture), in two lots, and blitz to a sauce, adding up to 300 ml of boiling water if too thick to pour. Pour into sterilized bottles. Seal, label, date and store in a cool place. Use within 12 months.

1 kg fresh plums, washed, halved and stones removed

500 g onions, chopped

8 cloves garlic, chopped

7.5 cm chunk fresh ginger, peeled and chopped

150 ml hot, fresh tea

600 ml malt vinegar

2 cinnamon sticks, crushed

2 tbsp five-spice powder

4 fresh red chillies, deseeded, chopped

450 g dark brown muscovado sugar

Makes 1.25 litres

This baked dessert originating from Limousin, in France, is rather like a sweet, slightly custardy type of Yorkshire pudding. It has fresh plums in it and a little fruit-scented eau-de-vie or brandy too. It is easy: make it using a blender and there's no whisking whatsoever. Bake the pudding in a fan-assisted oven. Serve it, hot and puffed, direct from the dish.

plum clafoutis

Have the fan-assisted oven preheated to 180°C. (If using a normal oven increase the heat by 20°C to 200°C, 400°F, Gas 6: it will not, however, be as crispy at the edges.)

Use the butter to generously grease a 1 litre capacity shallow metal, heatproof glass or ceramic dish about 23 cm diameter and no more than 3-4 cm deep. Put in ³/₄ of the plums. Scatter the icing sugar over them. Put the dish into the oven and cook for 10 minutes. Meanwhile combine the batter ingredients, in order, in a blender. Whiz for 30 seconds. Stop the blender once; scrape down any pockets of dry flour and whiz again for 20 seconds. This guarantees lump-free batter. Without removing the dish from the oven, slide the hot dish and oven shelf out far enough to pour over the batter. Add the remaining plums. Let the clafoutis cook for a further 40-45 minutes or until golden, puffed, juicy and aromatic. Serve it hot dusted with icing sugar.

Tip: Serve with chilled cream if liked.

15 g salted butter (for greasing the dish)

350 g plums, pitted (stoned) and quartered

3 tbsp icing sugar

¹/₂ tsp allspice

Batter:

3 eggs

250 ml milk

¹/₄ tsp salt

75 g plain flour

75 g caster or vanilla sugar

1 tbsp eau-de-vie schnapps such as slivovitz, kirsch, poire etc. or else dark rum

To decorate:

icing sugar, for dusting

Serves 6-8

cherries

The sight of a cherry orchard, first in blossom and then laden with fruit is truly nothing short of wonderful. They are one of the season's juiciest fruits and are delicious eaten shiny-bright and unadorned straight from the bowl. They also go well with Greek yogurt and fromage frais and cherry sauce can be served to turn a simple stand-by pudding into something really special. They can also be used as an accompaniment to rich meats including the classic duck combination.

Here is an ice cream for those who have no ice-cream maker or sorbetiere. Make it as soon as fresh cherries are on sale: buy twice what you need and enjoy half of them eaten raw, then make this ice cream with the remainder. Allow about 4-6 hours for it to freeze: it needs no stirring whatsoever.

cherry and almond ice cream

Use a cherry pitter or olive stoner to remove the cherry stones. (Use them, crushed, to flavour gin or vodka: they are far too good to waste.) Now sprinkle the cherries with the sugar, and the juice or water and cook, covered, over a moderate heat until the berries soften and give up some of their rich, red juice. Cool them over ice or stand the pan in iced water. Now whip the cream with the 4 tablespoons of the sweetened juice. Whip until soft peaks form. Mash the cherries. Fold them in. Pour ice cream into a 1-litre lidded freezer container. Label. Freeze 4-6 hours.

To serve: "condition" the ice cream for 40-50 minutes in the fridge. Serve in scoops or chunky blocks, or in cones.

Note: If no fresh cherries are available, use drained, canned cherries or preserved, bottled cherries in a kirsch-flavoured syrup instead; using the drained-off syrup as a drink.

350 g fresh cherries

75 g vanilla sugar

4 tbsp red summer fruits juice or water

450 ml double cream

$\frac{1}{2}$ tsp almond essence

Makes 1 litre

Gorgeous little open cherry pies, which have added marzipan to give the almondy fragrance that cherry kernels, when crushed, give, but without the effort. On the other hand, if you have the time, do crush 10 or so cherry stones, extract the white kernels and add them to this recipe: they are uniquely delicious. Make one large tart, if you prefer, not six.

cherry and marzipan tarts

Sweet short pastry:
175 g plain flour
50 g butter, softened and chopped
50 g icing sugar
1 medium egg
1 egg yolk
Or use 325 g bought sweet short pastry

Filling:
350 g fresh, ripe cherries, pitted (use a cherry stoner)
75 g almond marzipan
2 tsp custard powder
4 tbsp caster sugar
300 ml red fruits juice such as cherry, raspberry, etc.
1 tbsp fruit brandy (such as kirsch) or other fruit eau-de-vie

To serve:
vanilla custard, yogurt or crème fraîche (optional)

Makes 6 small x 10 cm diameter tarts
(or 1 x 23 cm diameter tart)

Have the oven preheated to 220°C, 425°F, Gas 7 and have ready 6 x 10 cm diameter metal flan tins (loose-based) or one large 23 cm diameter metal flan tin with a loose base. Put 150 g of the flour into a food processor with the butter, icing sugar, egg and egg yolk. Whiz, in brief bursts to make a soft, dense biscuity mass. Remove it from the processor. Work in the remaining 25 g flour by hand to make a firm, sweet dough. Plastic wrap it and chill for 30 minutes. Now divide the marzipan into eight equal portions. Cut each of these into 8 giving 64 pieces. Roll them into little balls. Push one inside each pitted cherry or else mix marzipan balls with the whole cherries, if they are unpitted. Unwrap the dough. Divide it into 6 equal portions and pat each into a circle. Roll into circles a little bigger than each flan tin. Lift and place the pastry circles into each flan tin; pastry is very soft, so if necessary, repair any tears by pushing the dough together. Push the dough to line them evenly. Prick all over with a fork. If using one large flan tin, line it with the pastry in the same way. Bake the pastry blind (no weights or foil are needed) for 15 minutes. Add the cherries and the marzipan. Bake for a further 20-25 minutes until the cherries are soft and juicy. Now mix the sugar and custard powder together and whisk into the cherry juice. Heat over high heat, stirring to make a glossy glaze. Cool slightly. Stir in the alcohol. Spoon or pour the glaze over the cherries. Serve hot, warm or cool with the accompaniment of your choice.

Tip: If using defrosted or bottle cherries, drain them well. Use any juice as the glaze liquid. If no eau-de-vie is available, substitute 1 teaspoon vanilla essence.

index